THE BATTLES WITH HAN

"In the annals of cinematic history, there are few figures as iconic, as influential, as deeply etched in the collective consciousness as Bruce Lee"

His unparalleled martial arts prowess, sheer screen presence, and philosophies have left a lasting legacy that continues to inspire and captivate audiences worldwide. The photo book you hold in your hands, "Battles with Han", is a tribute to one of Lee's most formidable adversaries and memorable on-screen battles in his career.

Han, a renegade Shaolin monk turned crime lord, stands as one of the most significant characters in martial arts cinema. His chilling portrayal, equipped with an artificial left hand that morphs into menacing weapons, created an antagonist worthy of Bruce Lee's hero. This book is a photographic journey into the tense, high-stakes duels between these two unique characters.
The first section of this collection showcases the initial encounter outside the cavern with Han's guards. Lee's fluid movements, lightning speed, and razor-sharp precision are immortalized in each photograph, giving you the chance to relive these incredible moments frame by frame.

The second half transports you to the final encounter in the trophy room. Here, the tension crescendos, and the stakes amplify. Bruce Lee armed with his skill, determination, and an unwavering sense of justice, goes up against Han's cunning, ruthlessness, and deadly mechanical hand. It's a clash of titans, a duel between good and evil, a battle that will decide the fate of many.

"Battles with Han" is more than just a collection of stunning photographs. It is a tribute to Bruce Lee's enduring legacy and an exploration of the archetypal battle between good and evil. It celebrates the artistry and athleticism that defined his career and forever changed the landscape of martial arts cinema.

Whether you're a long-standing Bruce Lee enthusiast or new to his timeless work, this book will invite you into the heart of the action, where you can experience the drama, the intensity, and the magic of these iconic battles. Let this journey with Bruce Lee remind you of his indomitable spirit, his unparalleled skill, and the timeless message of resilience and justice he left for the world.

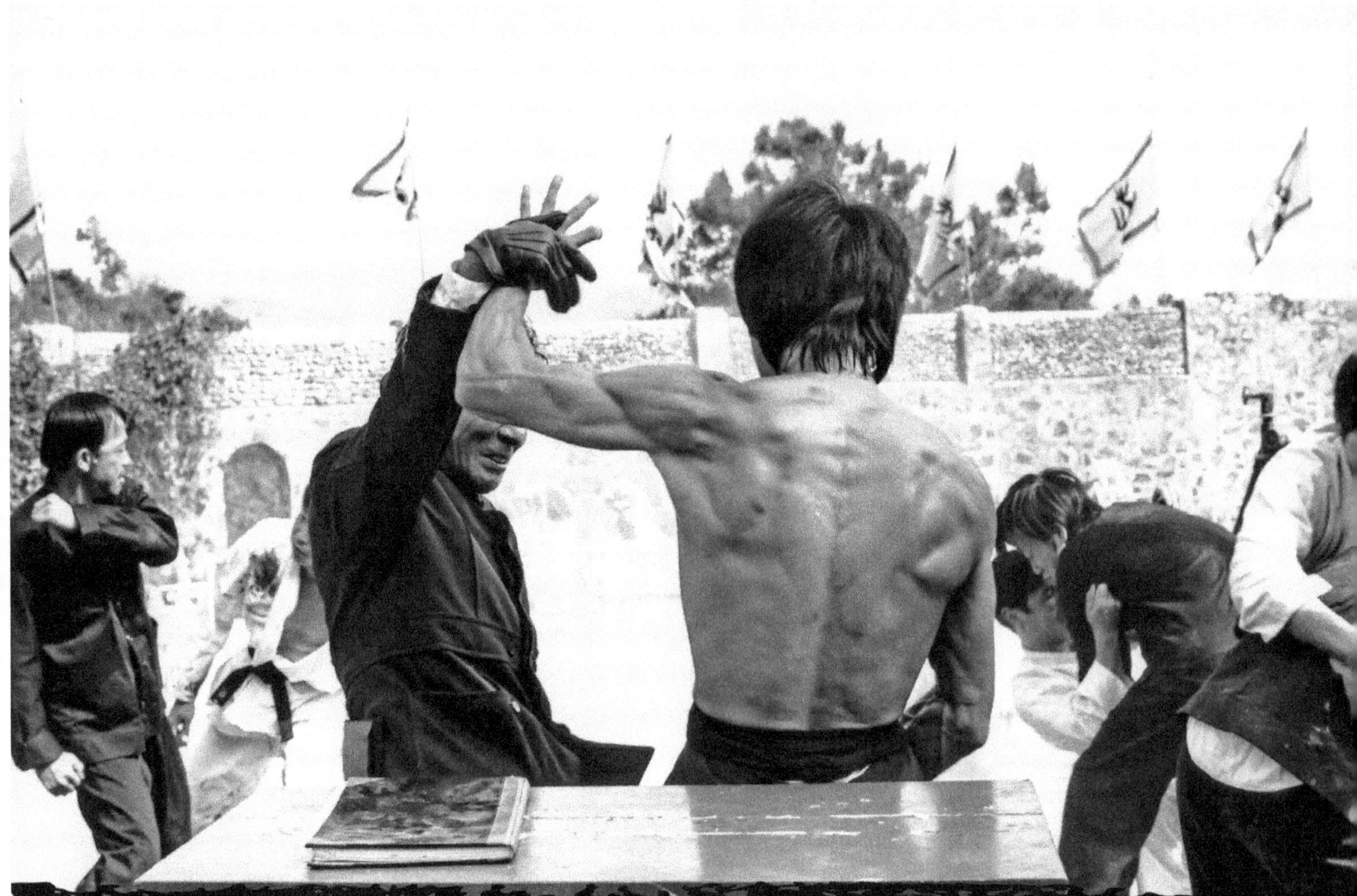

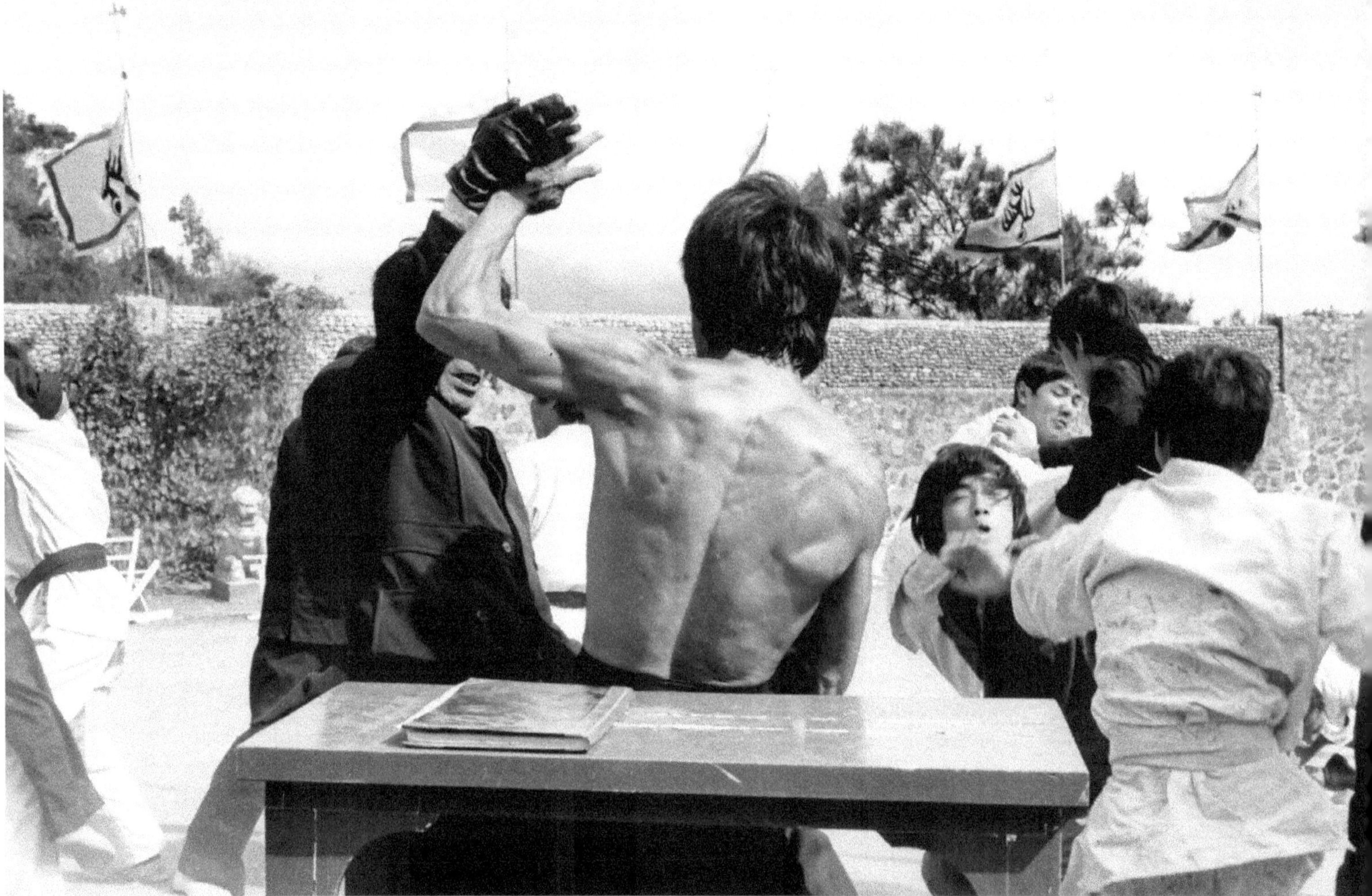

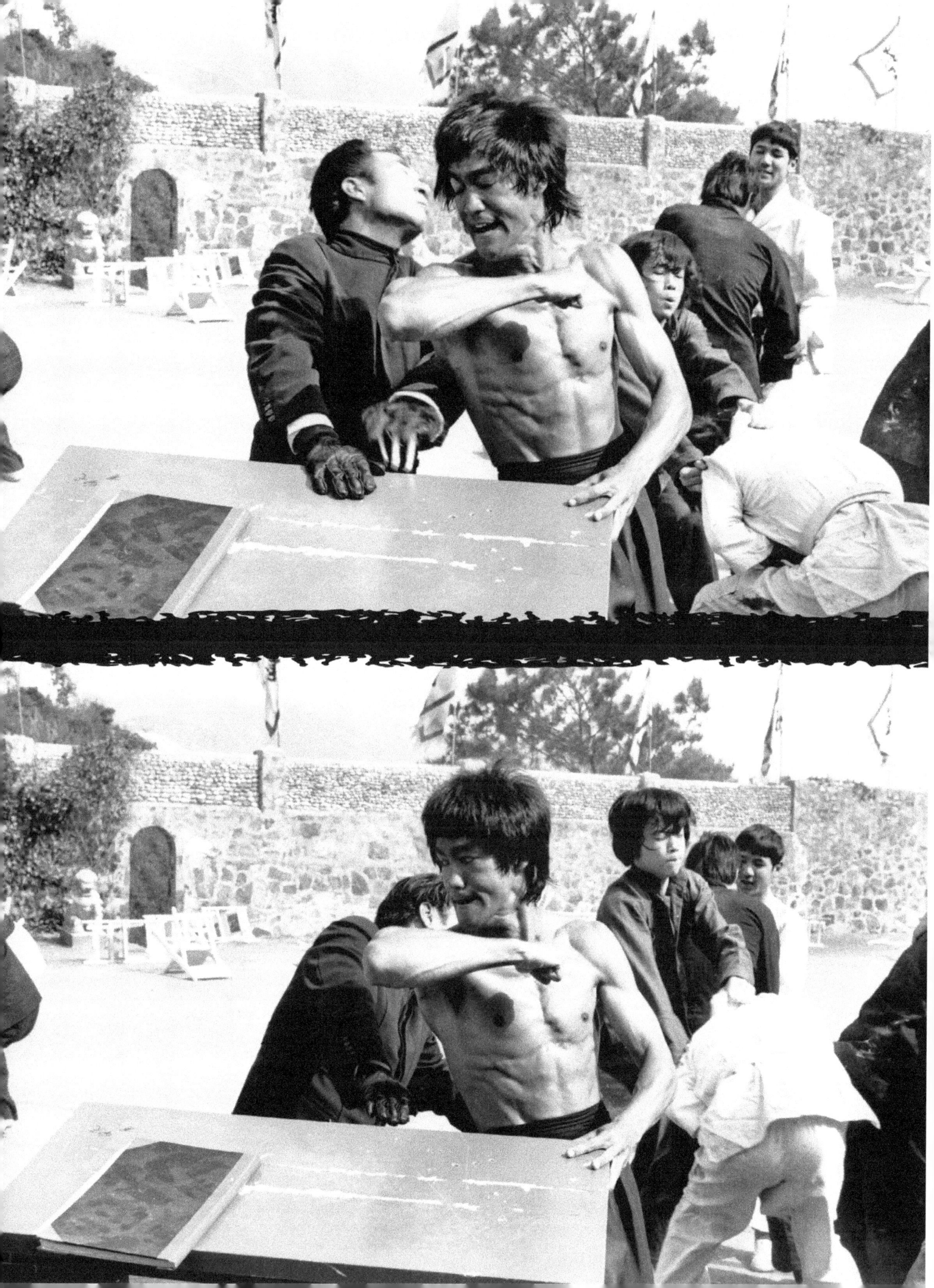

THE TROPHY ROOM

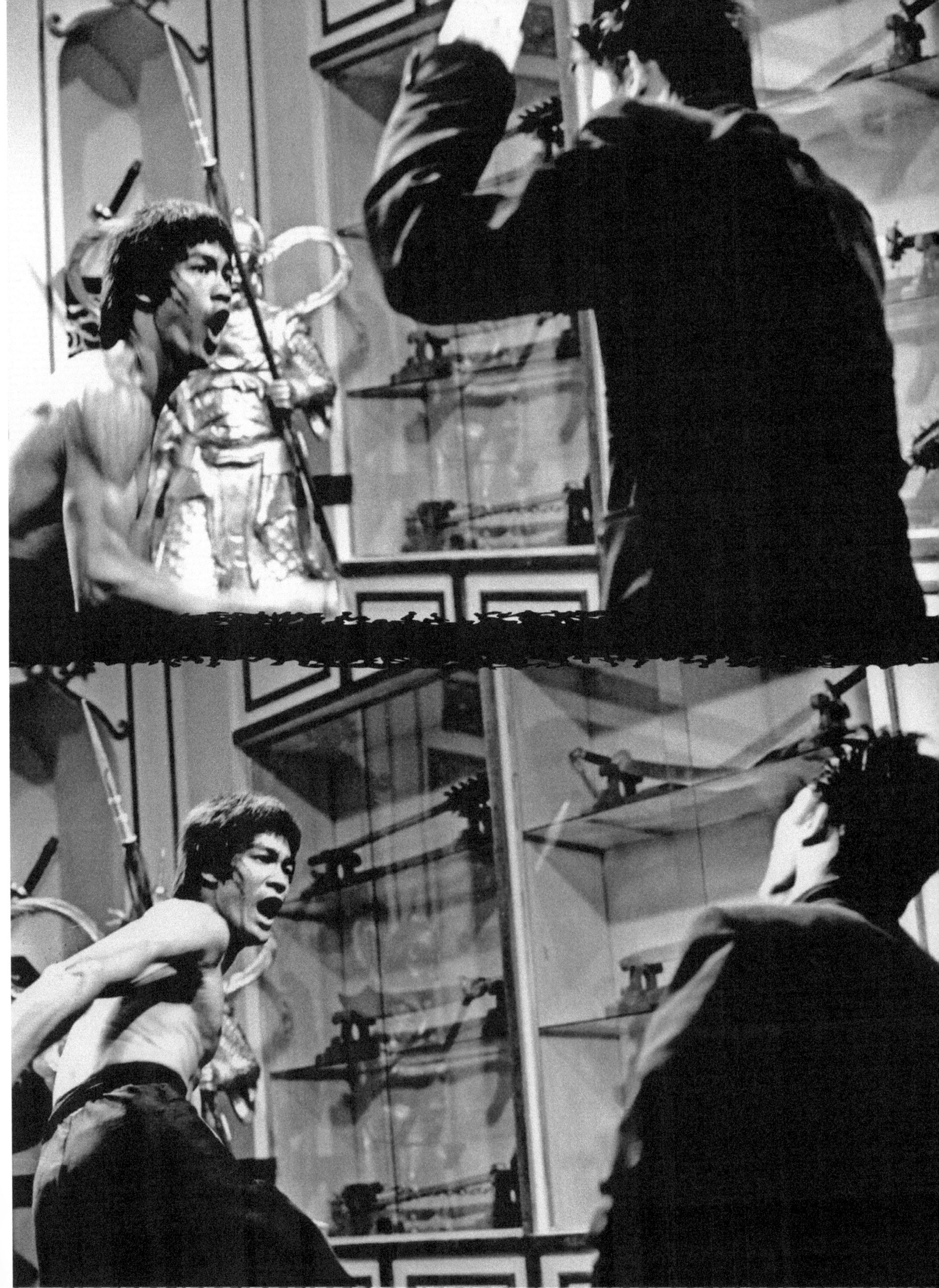

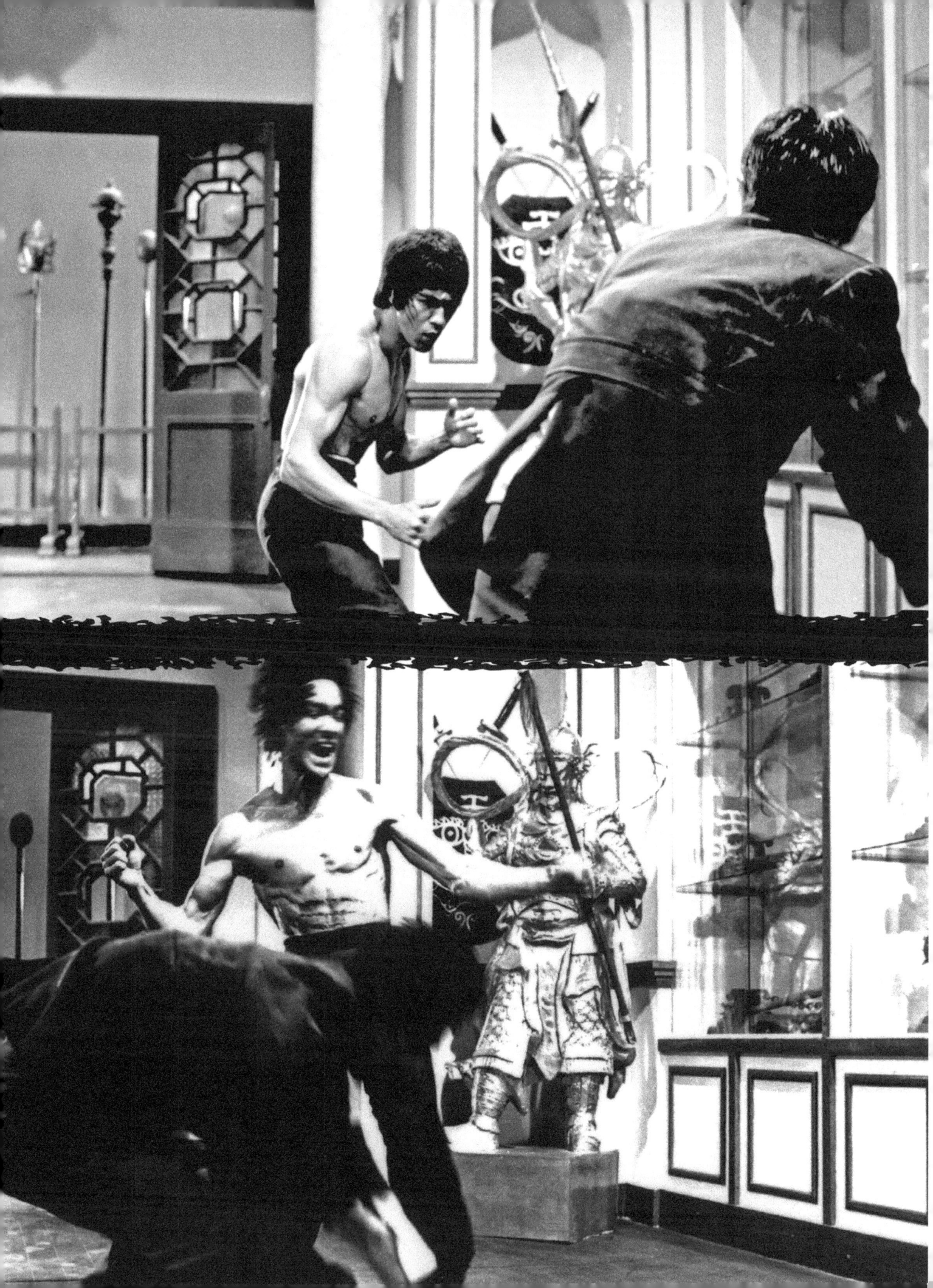

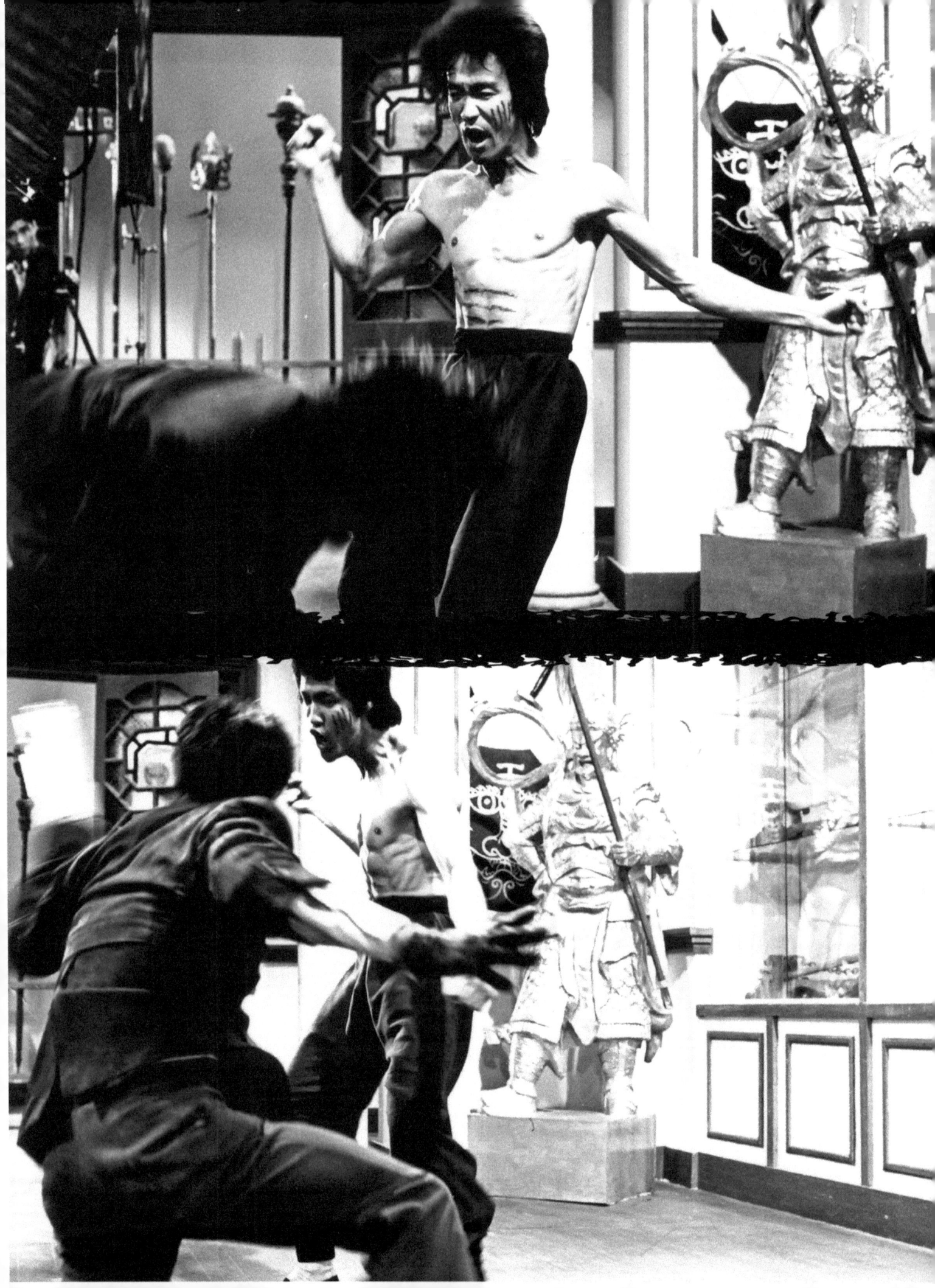

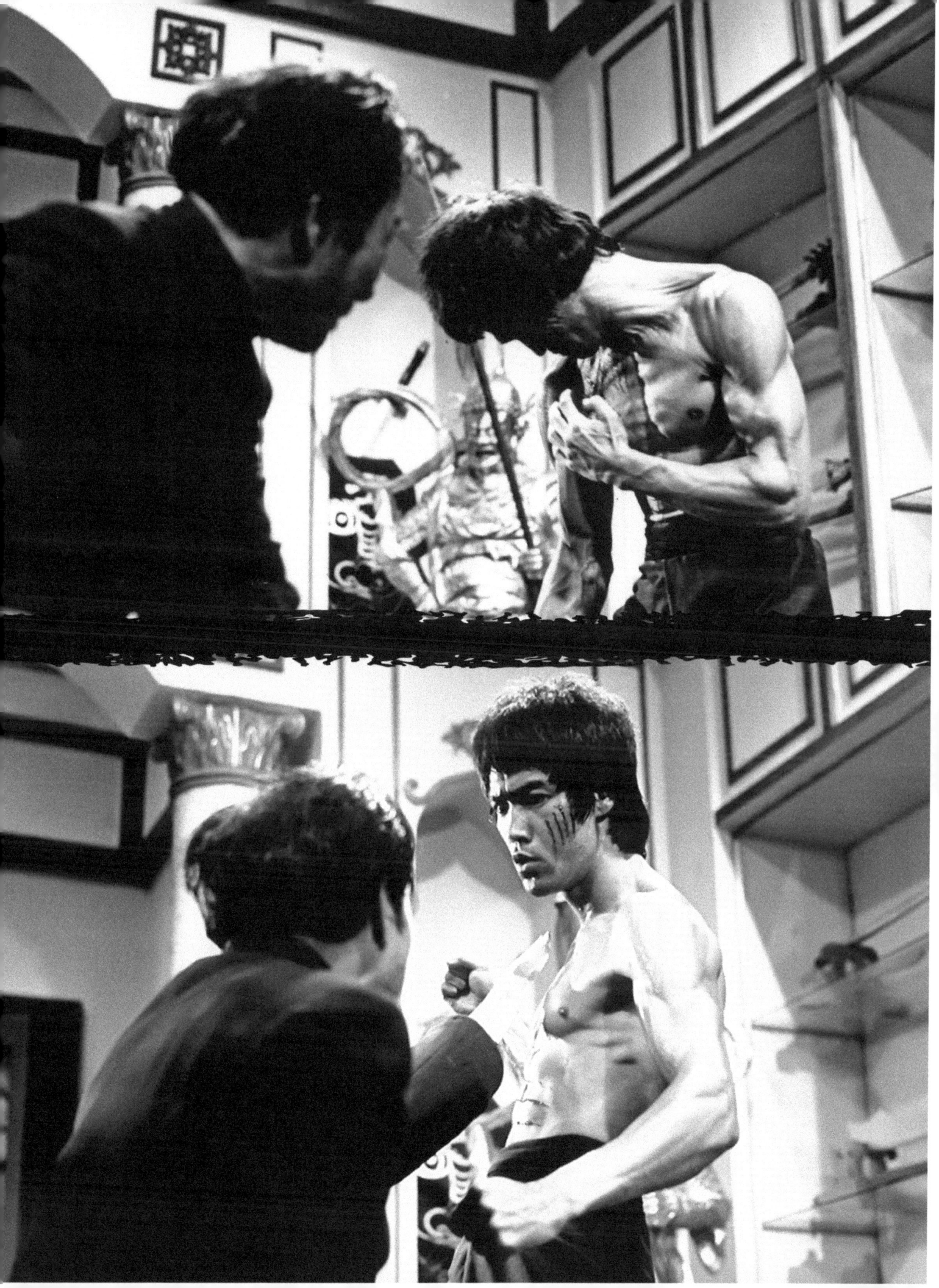

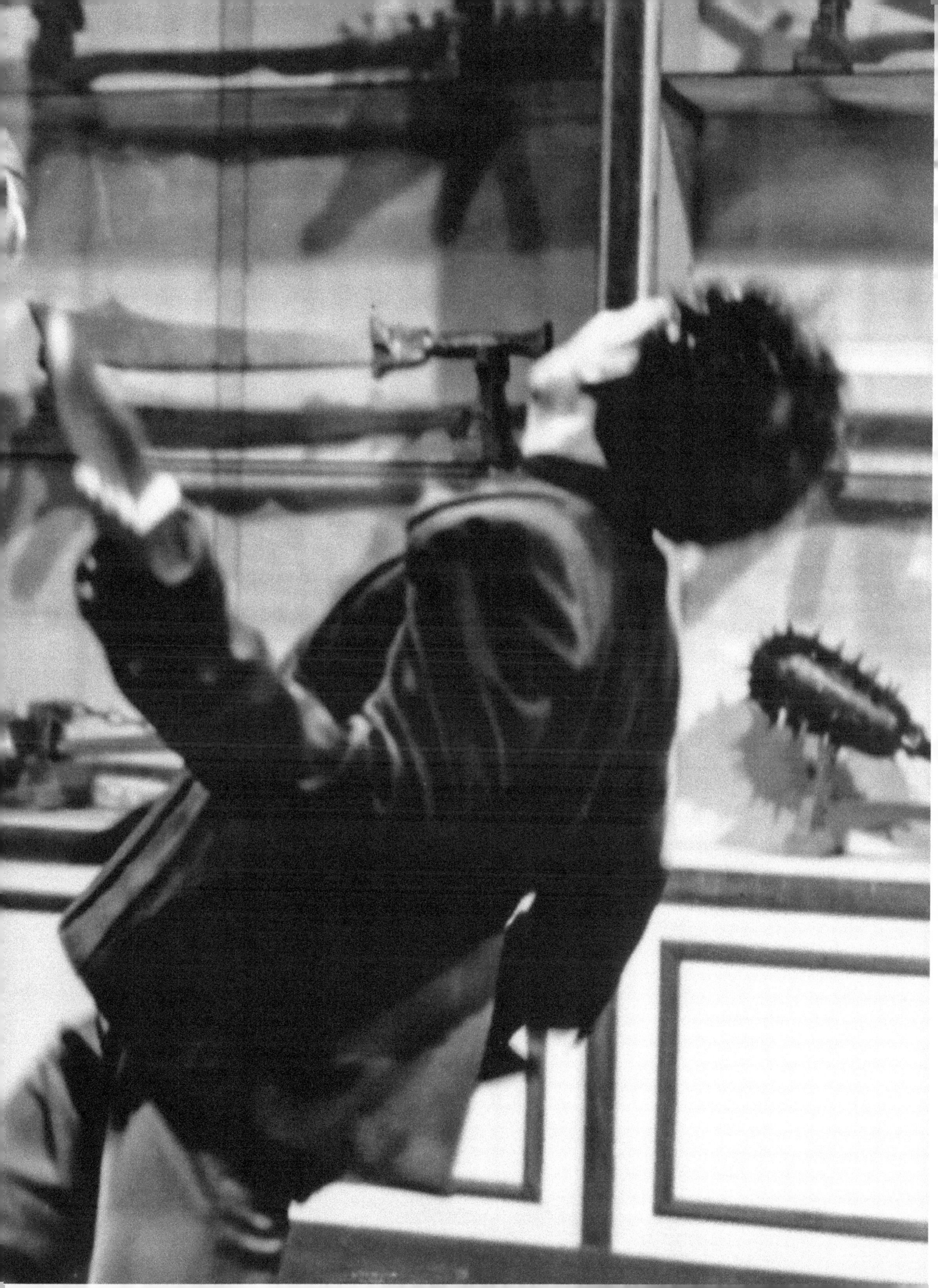

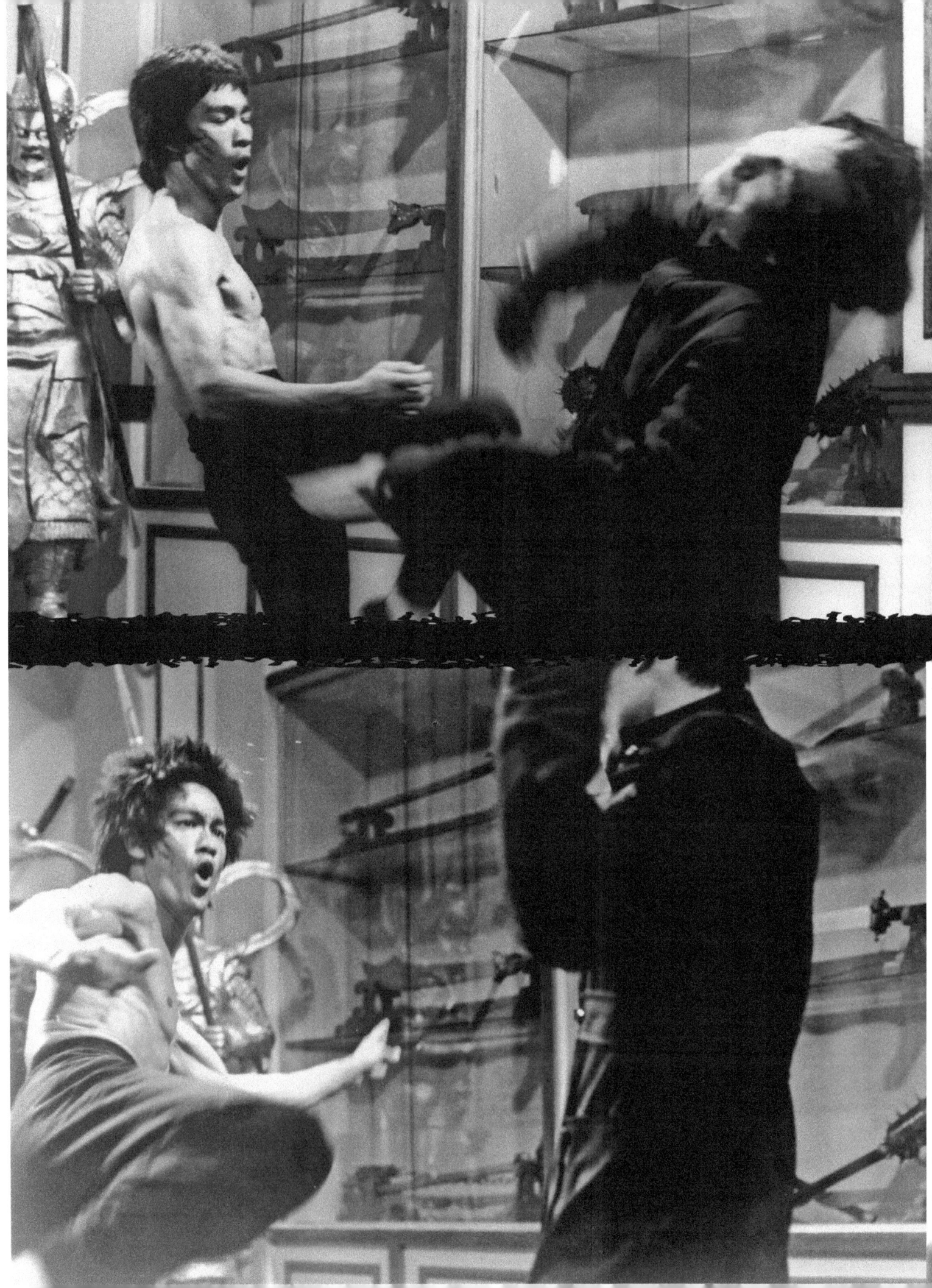

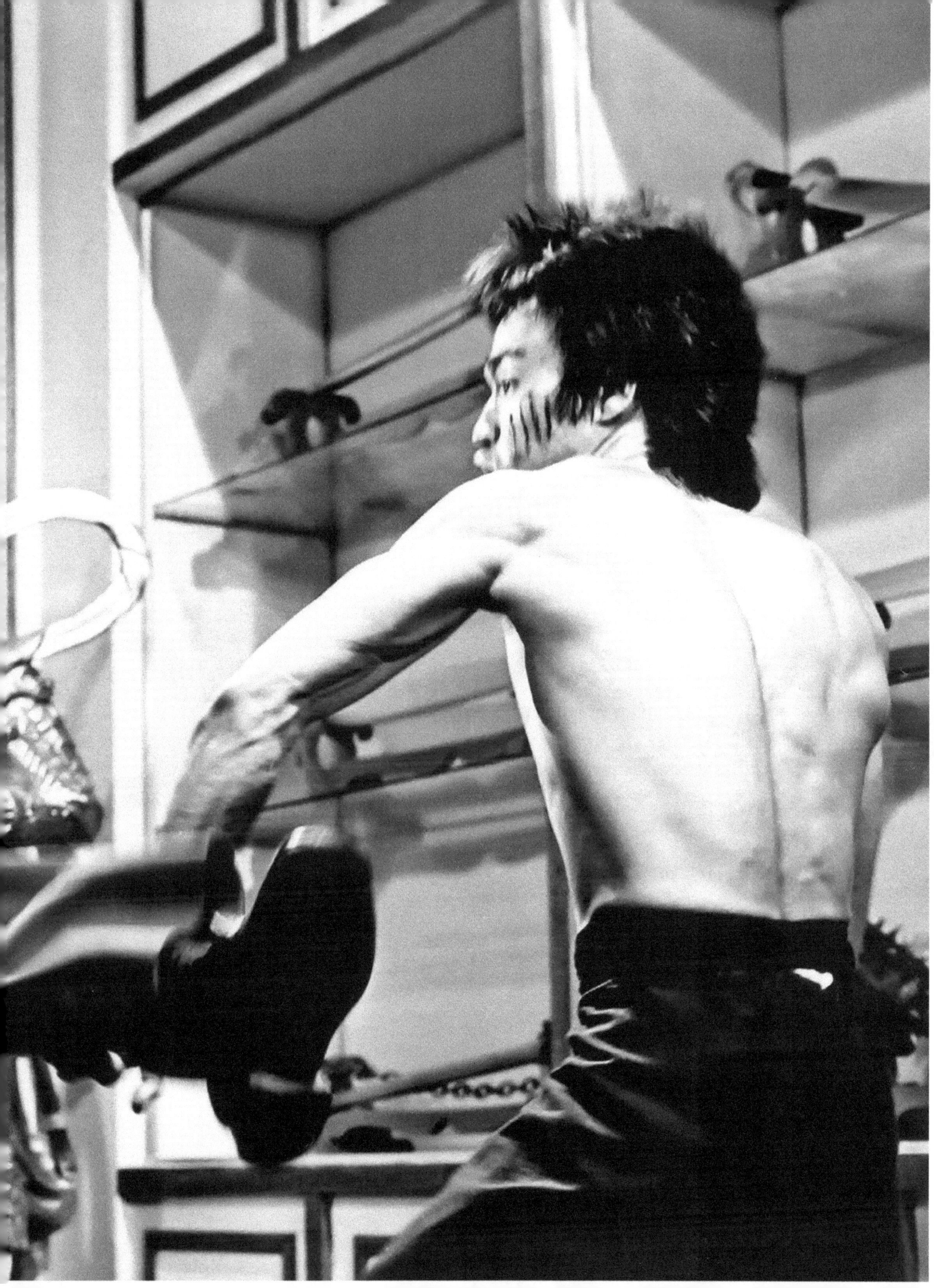

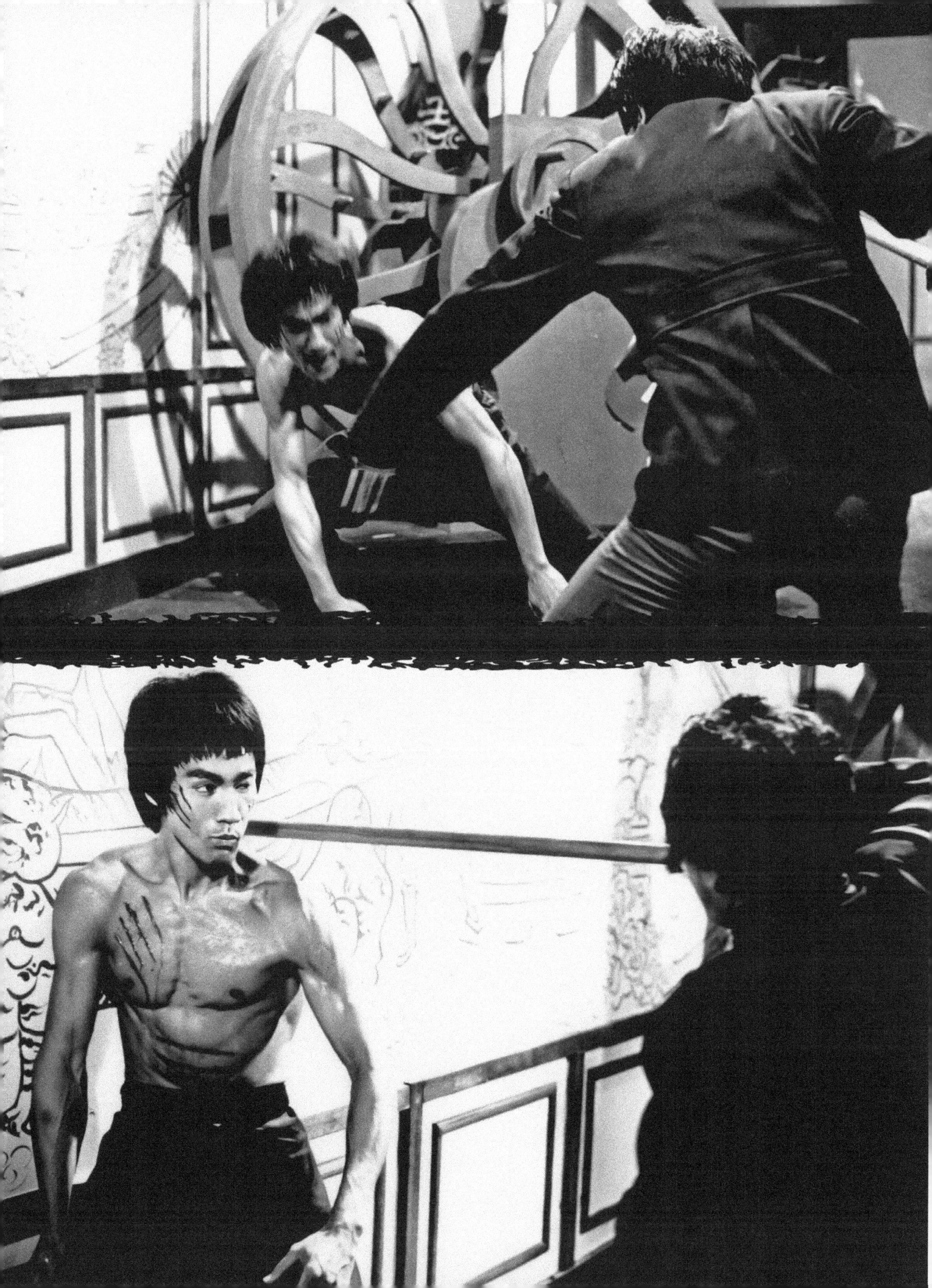

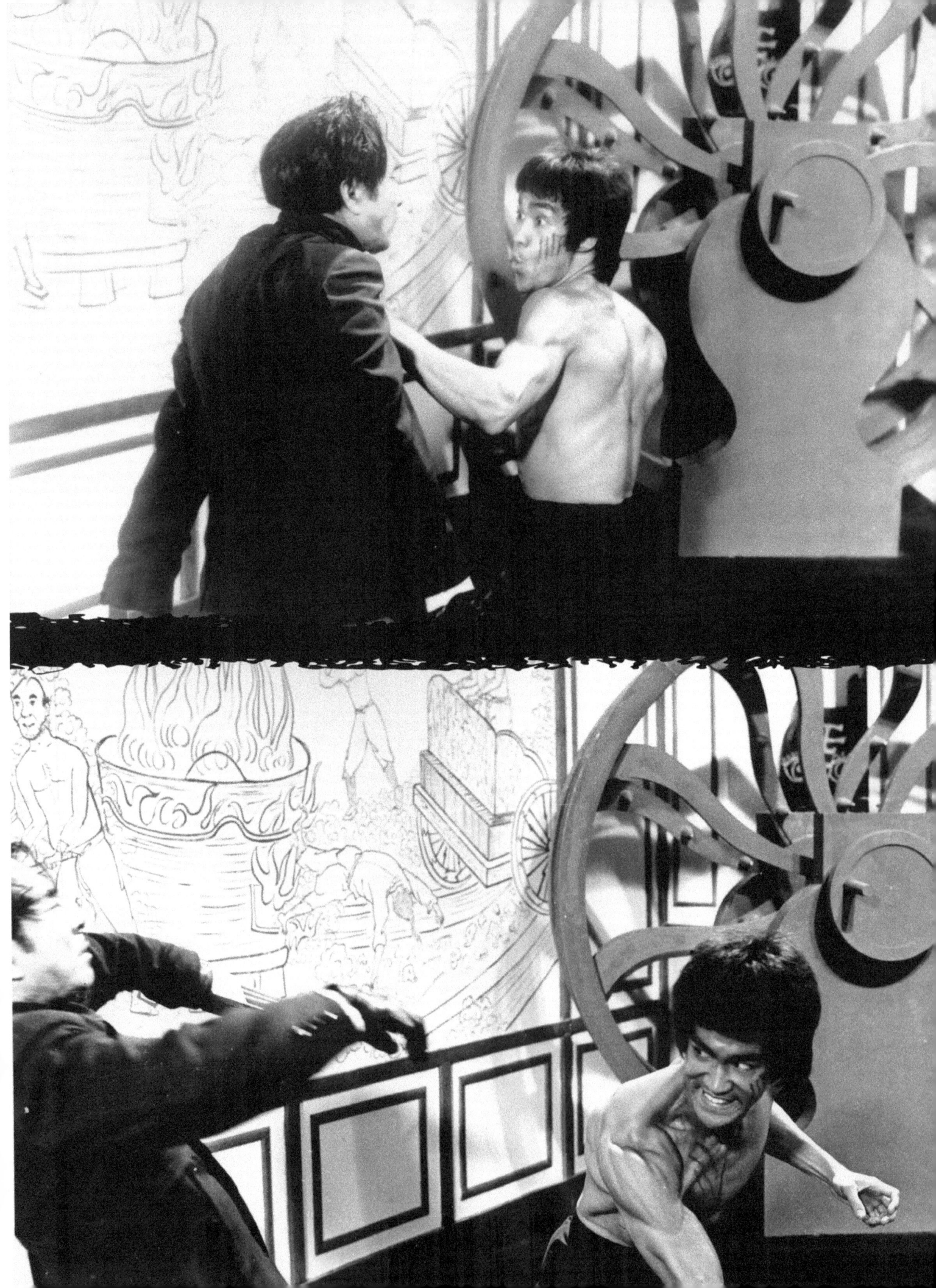

www.ingramcontent.com/pod-product-compliance
Lightning Source LLC
Chambersburg PA
CBHW042027100526
44587CB00029B/4322